Great Works
Instructional Guides for Literature

BRIDGE TO
TERABITHIA

A guide for the novel by Katherine Paterson
Great Works Author: Jessica Case, M.A.Ed.

SHELL EDUCATION

Publishing Credits

Kristy Stark, Editor

Image Credits

Shutterstock (cover, p. 12, p. 42); Emily R. Smith (p. 11)

Standards

© 2007 Teachers of English to Speakers of Other Languages, Inc. (TESOL)
© 2007 Board of Regents of the University of Wisconsin System. World-Class Instructional Design and Assessment (WIDA).
© Copyright 2010. National Governors Association Center for Best Practices and Council of Chief State School Officers. All rights reserved.

Shell Education

5301 Oceanus Drive
Huntington Beach, CA 92649-1030
http://www.shelleducation.com

ISBN 978-1-4258-8974-6

© 2015 Shell Educational Publishing, Inc.

Table of Contents

How to Use This Literature Guide

Today's standards demand rigor and relevance in the reading of complex texts. The units in this series guide teachers in a rich and deep exploration of worthwhile works of literature for classroom study. The most rigorous instruction can also be interesting and engaging!

Many current strategies for effective literacy instruction have been incorporated into these instructional guides for literature. Throughout the units, text-dependent questions are used to determine comprehension of the novel as well as student interpretation of the vocabulary words. The novels chosen for the series are complex exemplars of carefully crafted works of literature. Close reading is used throughout the units to guide students toward revisiting the text and using textual evidence to respond to prompts orally and in writing. Students must analyze the story elements in multiple assignments for each section of the novel. All of these strategies work together to rigorously guide students through their study of literature.

The next few pages will make clear how to use this guide for a purposeful and meaningful literature study. Each section of this guide is set up in the same way to make it easier for you to implement the instruction in your classroom.

Theme Thoughts

The great works of literature used throughout this series have important themes that have been relevant to people for many years. Many of the themes will be discussed during the various sections of this instructional guide. However, it would also benefit students to have independent time to think about the key themes of the novel.

Before students begin reading, have them complete *Pre-Reading Theme Thoughts* (page 13). This graphic organizer will allow students to think about the themes outside the context of the story. They'll have the opportunity to evaluate statements based on important themes and defend their opinions. Be sure to have students keep their papers for comparison to the *Post-Reading Theme Thoughts* (page 64). This graphic organizer is similar to the pre-reading activity. However, this time, students will be answering the questions from the point of view of one of the characters of the novel. They have to think about how the character would feel about each statement and defend their thoughts. To conclude the activity, have students compare what they thought about the themes before they read the novel to what the characters discovered during the story.

How to Use This Literature Guide *(cont.)*

Vocabulary

Each teacher overview page has definitions and sentences about how key vocabulary words are used in the section. These words should be introduced and discussed with students. There are two student vocabulary activity pages in each section. On the first page, students are asked to define the ten words chosen by the author of this unit. On the second page in most sections, each student will select at least eight words that he or she finds interesting or difficult. For each section, choose one of these pages for your students to complete. With either assignment, you may want to have students get into pairs to discuss the meanings of the words. Allow students to use reference guides to define the words. Monitor students to make sure the definitions they have found are accurate and relate to how the words are used in the text.

On some of the vocabulary student pages, students are asked to answer text-related questions about the vocabulary words. The following question stems will help you create your own vocabulary questions if you'd like to extend the discussion.

- How does this word describe _____'s character?
- In what ways does this word relate to the problem in this story?
- How does this word help you understand the setting?
- In what ways is this word related to the story's solution?
- Describe how this word supports the novel's theme of . . . .
- What visual images does this word bring to your mind?
- For what reasons might the author have chosen to use this particular word?

At times, more work with the words will help students understand their meanings. The following quick vocabulary activities are a good way to further study the words.

- Have students practice their vocabulary and writing skills by creating sentences and/or paragraphs in which multiple vocabulary words are used correctly and with evidence of understanding.
- Students can play vocabulary concentration. Students make a set of cards with the words and a separate set of cards with the definitions. Then, students lay the cards out on the table and play concentration. The goal of the game is to match vocabulary words with their definitions.
- Students can create word journal entries about the words. Students choose words they think are important and then describe why they think each word is important within the novel.

How to Use This Literature Guide *(cont.)*

Analyzing the Literature

After students have read each section, hold small-group or whole-class discussions. Questions are written at two levels of complexity to allow you to decide which questions best meet the needs of your students. The Level 1 questions are typically less abstract than the Level 2 questions. Level 1 is indicated by a square, while Level 2 is indicated by a triangle. These questions focus on the various story elements, such as character, setting, and plot. Student pages are provided if you want to assign these questions for individual student work before your group discussion. Be sure to add further questions as your students discuss what they've read. For each question, a few key points are provided for your reference as you discuss the novel with students.

Reader Response

In today's classrooms, there are often great readers who are below average writers. So much time and energy is spent in classrooms getting students to read on grade level, that little time is left to focus on writing skills. To help teachers include more writing in their daily literacy instruction, each section of this guide has a literature-based reader response prompt. Each of the three genres of writing is used in the reader responses within this guide: narrative, informative/explanatory, and argument. Students have a choice between two prompts for each reader response. One response requires students to make connections between the reading and their own lives. The other prompt requires students to determine text-to-text connections or connections within the text.

Close Reading the Literature

Within each section, students are asked to closely reread a short section of text. Since some versions of the novels have different page numbers, the selections are described by chapter and location, along with quotations to guide the readers. After each close reading, there are text-dependent questions to be answered by students.

Encourage students to read each question one at a time and then go back to the text and discover the answer. Work with students to ensure that they use the text to determine their answers rather than making unsupported inferences. Once students have answered the questions, discuss what they discovered. Suggested answers are provided in the answer key.

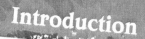

How to Use This Literature Guide *(cont.)*

Close Reading the Literature *(cont.)*

The generic, open-ended stems below can be used to write your own text-dependent questions if you would like to give students more practice.

- Give evidence from the text to support . . . .
- Justify your thinking using text evidence about . . . .
- Find evidence to support your conclusions about . . . .
- What text evidence helps the reader understand . . . ?
- Use the novel to tell why _____ happens.
- Based on events in the story, ...
- Use text evidence to describe why . . . .

Making Connections

The activities in this section help students make cross-curricular connections to writing, mathematics, science, social studies, or the fine arts. Each of these types of activities requires higher-order thinking skills from students.

Creating with the Story Elements

It is important to spend time discussing the common story elements in literature. Understanding the characters, setting, and plot can increase students' comprehension and appreciation of the story. If teachers discuss these elements daily, students will more likely internalize the concepts and look for the elements in their independent reading. Another important reason for focusing on the story elements is that students will be better writers if they think about how the stories they read are constructed.

Students are given three options for working with the story elements. They are asked to create something related to the characters, setting, or plot of the novel. Students are given a choice on this activity so that they can decide to complete the activity that most appeals to them. Different multiple intelligences are used so that the activities are diverse and interesting to all students.

How to Use This Literature Guide (cont.)

Culminating Activity

This open-ended, cross-curricular activity requires higher-order thinking and allows for a creative product. Students will enjoy getting the chance to share what they have discovered through reading the novel. Be sure to allow them enough time to complete the activity at school or home.

Comprehension Assessment

The questions in this section are modeled after current standardized tests to help students analyze what they've read and prepare for tests they may see in their classrooms. The questions are dependent on the text and require critical-thinking skills to answer.

Response to Literature

The final post-reading activity is an essay based on the text that also requires further research by students. This is a great way to extend this novel into other curricular areas. A suggested rubric is provided for teacher reference.

Correlation to the Standards

Shell Education is committed to producing educational materials that are research and standards based. As part of this effort, we have correlated all of our products to the academic standards of all 50 states, the District of Columbia, the Department of Defense Dependents Schools, and all Canadian provinces.

Purpose and Intent of Standards

Standards are designed to focus instruction and guide adoption of curricula. Standards are statements that describe the criteria necessary for students to meet specific academic goals. They define the knowledge, skills, and content students should acquire at each level. Standards are also used to develop standardized tests to evaluate students' academic progress. Teachers are required to demonstrate how their lessons meet standards. Standards are used in the development of all of our products, so educators can be assured they meet high academic standards.

How to Find Standards Correlations

To print a customized correlation report of this product for your state, visit our website at http://www.shelleducation.com and follow the online directions. If you require assistance in printing correlation reports, please contact our Customer Service Department at 1-877-777-3450.

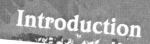

Correlation to the Standards (cont.)

Standards Correlation Chart

The lessons in this guide were written to support the Common Core College and Career Readiness Anchor Standards. This chart indicates which sections of this guide address the anchor standards.

Common Core College and Career Readiness Anchor Standard	Section
CCSS.ELA-Literacy.CCRA.R.1—Read closely to determine what the text says explicitly and to make logical inferences from it; cite specific textual evidence when writing or speaking to support conclusions drawn from the text.	Close Reading the Literature Sections 1–5; Creating with the Story Elements Sections 1–5; Making Connections Sections 2, 4; Culminating Activity
CCSS.ELA-Literacy.CCRA.R.2—Determine central ideas or themes of a text and analyze their development; summarize the key supporting details and ideas.	Analyzing the Literature Sections 1–5; Reader Response Sections 1–5; Making Connections Section 5; Post-Reading Theme Thoughts
CCSS.ELA-Literacy.CCRA.R.3—Analyze how and why individuals, events, or ideas develop and interact over the course of a text.	Analyzing the Literature Sections 1-5; Reader Response Sections 1–5; Creating with the Story Elements Sections 1–5
CCSS.ELA-Literacy.CCRA.R.4—Interpret words and phrases as they are used in a text, including determining technical, connotative, and figurative meanings, and analyze how specific word choices shape meaning or tone.	Vocabulary Sections 1–5
CCSS.ELA-Literacy.CCRA.R.10—Read and comprehend complex literary and informational texts independently and proficiently.	Entire Unit
CCSS.ELA-Literacy.CCRA.W.1—Write arguments to support claims in an analysis of substantive topics or texts using valid reasoning and relevant and sufficient evidence.	Reader Response Sections 2–4; Post-Reading Response to Literature
CCSS.ELA-Literacy.CCRA.W.2—Write informative/explanatory texts to examine and convey complex ideas and information clearly and accurately through the effective selection, organization, and analysis of content.	Reader Response Sections 1–2, 5; Post-Reading Response to Literature
CCSS.ELA-Literacy.CCRA.W.3—Write narratives to develop real or imagined experiences or events using effective technique, well-chosen details and well-structured event sequences.	Reader Response Sections 1, 3–5; Creating with the Story Elements Sections 3–4; Making Connections Section 4; Culminating Activity
CCSS.ELA-Literacy.CCRA.W.4—Produce clear and coherent writing in which the development, organization, and style are appropriate to task, purpose, and audience.	Reader Response Sections 1–5; Creating with the Story Elements Sections 3–5; Making Connections Section 4; Culminating Activity; Post-Reading Response to Literature

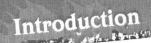

Correlation to the Standards (cont.)

Standards Correlation Chart (cont.)

Common Core College and Career Readiness Anchor Standard	Section
CCSS.ELA-Literacy.CCRA.W.7—Conduct short as well as more sustained research projects based on focused questions, demonstrating understanding of the subject under investigation.	Post-Reading Response to Literature
CCSS.ELA-Literacy.CCRA.SL.1—Prepare for and participate effectively in a range of conversations and collaborations with diverse partners, building on others' ideas and expressing their own clearly and persuasively.	Entire Unit
CCSS.ELA-Literacy.CCRA.L.1—Demonstrate command of the conventions of standard English grammar and usage when writing or speaking.	Analyzing the Literature Sections 1–5; Close Reading the Literature Sections 1–5; Reader Response Sections 1–5; Post-Reading Response to Literature
CCSS.ELA-Literacy.CCRA.L.2—Demonstrate command of the conventions of standard English capitalization, punctuation, and spelling when writing.	Analyzing the Literature Sections 1–5; Close Reading the Literature Sections 1–5; Reader Response Sections 1–5; Post-Reading Response to Literature
CCSS.ELA-Literacy.CCRA.L.4—Determine or clarify the meaning of unknown and multiple-meaning words and phrases by using context clues, analyzing meaningful word parts, and consulting general and specialized reference materials, as appropriate.	Vocabulary Sections 1–5
CCSS.ELA-Literacy.CCRA.L.6—Acquire and use accurately a range of general academic and domain-specific words and phrases sufficient for reading, writing, speaking, and listening at the college and career readiness level; demonstrate independence in gathering vocabulary knowledge when encountering an unknown term important to comprehension or expression.	Vocabulary Sections 1–5

TESOL and WIDA Standards

The lessons in this book promote English language development for English language learners. The following TESOL and WIDA English Language Development Standards are addressed through the activities in this book:

- **Standard 1:** English language learners communicate for social and instructional purposes within the school setting.

- **Standard 2:** English language learners communicate information, ideas and concepts necessary for academic success in the content area of language arts.

About the Author—Katherine Paterson

Katherine Paterson was born in China in 1932 as Katherine Womeldorf. Her family moved 13 times in 13 years because of her father's job and the ongoing war in China. Once her family settled down in the United States, Katherine graduated from King College in Bristol, Tennessee, summa cum laude with an English degree. She spent her first year as a teacher in a rural elementary school in Virginia. This setting was the inspiration for *Bridge to Terabithia*. She went on to get her master's degree in Bible and Christian education from the Presbyterian School of Christian Education in Richmond, Virginia.

She dreamed of going back to China to be a missionary. However, the borders were closed to Western citizens at the time, so she went to Japan. She enjoyed every aspect of Japan, as she worked and lived there as a missionary for four years. She planned to stay in Japan but returned to the United States to study for a year in New York. While there she met and fell in love with a Presbyterian pastor, and they were married in 1962.

In 1964 her writing career took off when the Presbyterian Church asked her to write fifth and sixth grade curriculum. By the time the curriculum was published, she had become immersed in writing and in being a mother of three. She eventually began writing more fiction than nonfiction because she loved to read fiction. While balancing being a mother and working, she tried, unsuccessfully, to write and publish fictional stories. Her friend persuaded her to take a creative writing class. The novel she wrote in that class was published, and she finally felt like a writer. She writes her novels from home and enjoys visiting schools where she meets people who are as enthusiastic about reading and writing as she is.

Possible Texts for Text Comparisons

A similar novel to *Bridge to Terabithia* is *Jacob Have I Loved*. The story takes place near the Chesapeake Bay and tells of a relationship between twin sisters, Caroline and Louise, and their family and friends.

Book Summary of *Bridge to Terabithia*

Bridge to Terabithia tells the story of an unlikely friendship between a city girl and a country boy. Jess has trained all summer to be the fastest boy in the fifth grade, only to get beat by none other than a new girl named Leslie. Leslie is from the city, and she is Jess's new neighbor. In an unlikely event, Jess sticks up for Leslie and the two become friends. Jess shows Leslie the life of a rural farm town, while Leslie shows Jess the wonderful world of imagination, known as Terabithia. While in their imaginative and magical world of Terabithia, Jess and Leslie rule over all the land, which includes the evergreens and squirrels. They keep Terabithia safe from the bullies and real-life situations that occur at home and at school. It's only when an accident occurs that Jess must come to terms with what's real and what's imaginative. He struggles to keep Terabithia alive, while everything else around him has changed forever.

Cross-Curricular Connection

This novel can be used during a social studies unit on rural, urban, and suburban communities. It can also be used to discuss and study friendships and relationships.

Possible Texts for Text Sets

- Lewis, C.S. *The Lion, the Witch and the Wardrobe*. HarperCollins, 2002.
- Rylant, Cynthia. *Missing May*. Scholastic Paperbacks, 2004.
- Cleary, Beverly. *Dear Mr. Henshaw*. HarperCollins, 2009.

Name _____

Date _____

Pre-Reading Theme Thoughts

Directions: Read each of the statements in the first column. Decide if you agree or disagree with the statements. Record your opinion by marking an X in Agree or Disagree for each statement. Explain your choices in the fourth column. There are no right or wrong answers.

Statement	Agree	Disagree	Explain Your Answer
People from different backgrounds can become best friends.	✓		
There is no place for imagination in everyday living.		✓	
People can overcome tragedies.	✓		
Certain mistakes cannot be forgiven.	✓		

Vocabulary Overview

Ten key words from this section are provided below with definitions and sentences about how the words are used in the novel. Choose one of the vocabulary activity sheets (pages 15 or 16) for students to complete as they read this section. Monitor students as they work to ensure the definitions they have found are accurate and relate to the text. Finally, discuss these important vocabulary words with students. If you think these words or other words in the section warrant more time devoted to them, there are suggestions in the introduction for other vocabulary activities (page 5).

Word	Definition	Sentence about Text
despise (ch. 1)	hate; dislike something very much	Jess **despises** the way his older sisters dressed him up when he was little.
rut (ch. 1)	a groove or indent in the earth	The boys create a **rut** in the ground to mark the finish line.
peculiar (ch. 1)	unusual or odd	Jess finds it **peculiar** that someone is moving into the Perkins house.
muddled (ch. 2)	confused and vague	Jess tries to leave his **muddled** thoughts behind as he runs.
endure (ch. 2)	tolerate; *accept*	Music class on Fridays helps Jess **endure** the school week.
pandemonium (ch. 2)	chaos; disorder	The teachers do not like the **pandemonium** during music class.
proverbial (ch. 2)	familiar; well-known	Miss Edmunds calls Jess a **proverbial** diamond in the rough.
primly (ch. 3)	dainty or refined	The other girls in class are dressed more **primly** than Leslie for the first day of school.
conspicuous (ch. 3)	very obvious	The younger boys are **conspicuous** as they try to be included in the race.
conceited (ch. 3)	having an ~~exaggerated~~ *big; increased* sense of self-importance	Jess tries not to be **conceited** as he checks out his competition.

Name _____

Date _____

Understanding Vocabulary Words

Directions: The following words appear in this section of the novel. Use context clues and reference materials to determine an accurate definition for each word.

Word	Definition
despise (ch. 1)	
rut (ch. 1)	
peculiar (ch. 1)	
muddled (ch. 2)	
endure (ch. 2)	
pandemonium (ch. 2)	
proverbial (ch. 2)	
primly (ch. 3)	
conspicuous (ch. 3)	
conceited (ch. 3)	

Name _____

Date _____

During-Reading Vocabulary Activity

Directions: As you read these chapters, record at least eight important words on the lines below. Try to find interesting, difficult, intriguing, special, or funny words. Your words can be long or short. They can be hard or easy to spell. After each word, use context clues in the text and reference materials to define the word.

- _____
- _____
- _____
- _____
- _____
- _____
- _____
- _____
- _____
- _____

Directions: Respond to these questions about the words in this section.

1. In what ways does Jess **despise** his older sisters?

_____

_____

2. How is Leslie **conspicuous** as she enters the race in chapter 3?

_____

_____

_____

Analyzing the Literature

Provided below are discussion questions you can use in small groups, with the whole class, or for written assignments. Each question is given at two levels so you can choose the right question for each group of students. Activity sheets with these questions are provided (pages 18–19) if you want students to write their responses. For each question, a few key discussion points are provided for your reference.

Story Element	■ Level 1	▲ Level 2	Key Discussion Points
Character	Describe Jesse Oliver Aarons Jr.	How is Jess different from his sisters?	Jess is a quiet boy who likes to draw. He does chores around the house and wants to be the fastest runner at school. Jess gets up early to run and milk the cow, while Jess's sisters are lazy and get out of helping around the house. His sisters are also loud and whiny to get their way with his mother.
Setting	Describe the areas where students play at recess.	Explain how the recess areas lead to the boys' races.	The older boys play ball in the center of the upper field. The girls use the top section for hopscotch and jump rope. The lower field is the only area left for the younger boys. This area is either muddy or filled with deep ruts so the area isn't good for anything except running.
Character	Who is Leslie Burke?	Why does Jess dislike Leslie?	Leslie is a new girl at school, and she is Jess's neighbor. Leslie becomes the fastest runner in the fifth grade. This upsets Jess because he has been training to win the race.
Plot	What is the procedure for the races at recess?	How does Leslie change the mood of the race?	Gary Fulcher numbers off the boys into heats. The winners from each heat race in the final race. A girl has never participated in the races, let alone a girl who can run faster than all the boys. The boys are upset about losing to a girl.

Name _____

Date _____

▮ Analyzing the Literature

Directions: Think about the section you just read. Read each question and state your response with textual evidence.

1. Describe Jesse Oliver Aarons Jr.

   _____

   _____

   _____

2. Describe the areas where students play at recess.

   _____

   _____

   _____

3. Who is Leslie Burke?

   _____

   _____

   _____

4. What is the procedure for the races at recess?

   _____

   _____

   _____

Name _____

Date _____

▲ Analyzing the Literature

Directions: Think about the section you just read. Read each question and state your response with textual evidence.

1. How is Jess different from his sisters?

   _____

   _____

   _____

   _____

2. Explain how the recess areas lead to the boys' races.

   _____

   _____

   _____

   _____

3. Why does Jess dislike Leslie?

   _____

   _____

   _____

   _____

4. How does Leslie change the mood of the race?

   _____

   _____

   _____

   _____

Name _____

Date _____

Reader Response

Directions: Choose one of the following prompts about this section to answer. Be sure you include a topic sentence in your response, use textual evidence to support your opinion, and provide a strong conclusion that summarizes your opinion.

Writing Prompts

- **Narrative Piece**—Think about how Jess spends his summer vacation. If you could do anything for your summer vacation, what would you like to do? Write about your ideal summer vacation.
- **Informative/Explanatory Piece**—What questions are forming in your mind about Leslie Burke at this point? Write at least two questions and explain why you are curious about the answers.

_____

_____

_____

_____

_____

_____

_____

_____

_____

_____

_____

_____

_____

_____

Name _____

Date _____

Close Reading the Literature

Directions: Closely reread the section where Leslie joins the race during recess. Start toward the end of chapter 3 where it states, "Leslie lined up beside him on the right . . . ." Continue reading to the end of the chapter. Read each question and then revisit the text to find evidence that supports your answer.

1. What text evidence suggests that Jess is not thrilled with Leslie winning the race?

_____

_____

_____

2. Give evidence from the text to describe how Leslie feels when she wins the race during recess.

_____

_____

_____

3. Based on the text, how does Leslie's winning impact her relationship with Jess?

_____

_____

_____

4. Use the novel to describe how Jess uses Leslie in his ongoing struggle with Gary Fulcher.

_____

_____

_____

Name _____

Date _____

Making Connections—Chores

Directions: Jess Aarons spends most of his time during the summer doing chores and running. Create a poster that will help motivate Jess to get his chores done so he can practice what is most important to him—running.

Creating with the Story Elements

Directions: Thinking about the story elements of character, setting, and plot in a novel is very important to understanding what is happening and why. Complete **one** of the following activities based on what you've read so far. Be creative and have fun!

Characters

Draw a picture of Leslie on her first day of school. Include specific details to show how the text describes Leslie.

Setting

Create a map of the setting so far. Your map should include the Aarons' house, barn, and yard. Also include the school. Label the map.

Plot

Create a cause-and-effect flow chart. Place an event in a box, list what caused it, and what effect it had. Then, make a prediction as to what might happen next.

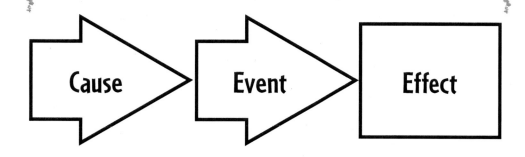

Vocabulary Overview

Ten key words from this section are provided below with definitions and sentences about how the words are used in the novel. Choose one of the vocabulary activity sheets (pages 25 or 26) for students to complete as they read this section. Monitor students as they work to ensure the definitions they have found are accurate and relate to the text. Finally, discuss these important vocabulary words with students. If you think these words or other words in the section warrant more time devoted to them, there are suggestions in the introduction for other vocabulary activities (page 5).

Word	Definition	Sentence about Text
consolation (ch. 4)	comfort; relief	Jess's only **consolation** about not winning the race is that Gary Fulcher doesn't win either.
melodic (ch. 4)	containing a pleasing melody	Miss Edmunds's **melodic** voice gives Jess a warm feeling inside.
deliberately (ch. 4)	carefully thought out	During music class, Jess **deliberately** chooses to change his feelings about Leslie.
consolidated (ch. 4)	combined	All students from the town are **consolidated** into one high school.
ominously (ch. 4)	threateningly	Leslie's **ominous** glance tells Jess to leave her alone.
gully (ch. 4)	deep ditch cut by running water	Jess and Leslie jump over a **gully** as they run into the woods.
stronghold (ch. 4)	a building or structure that is safe from attack	Jess and Leslie build a **stronghold** in Terabithia.
vigorously (ch. 4)	energetically	May Belle dances **vigorously** as Leslie and Jess decide how to get back at Janice Avery.
veiled (ch. 4)	concealed; hidden	The stronghold is **veiled** from intruders.
stricken (ch. 5)	overwhelmed by emotion	Janice Avery is **stricken** with anger after finding out Willard Hughes doesn't like her.

Name _____

Date _____

Understanding Vocabulary Words

Directions: The following words appear in this section of the novel. Use context clues and reference materials to determine an accurate definition for each word.

Word	Definition
consolation (ch. 4)	
melodic (ch. 4)	
deliberately (ch. 4)	
consolidated (ch. 4)	
ominously (ch. 4)	
gully (ch. 4)	
stronghold (ch. 4)	
vigorously (ch. 4)	
veiled (ch. 4)	
stricken (ch. 5)	

Name _____

Date _____

During-Reading Vocabulary Activity

Directions: As you read these chapters, record at least eight important words on the lines below. Try to find interesting, difficult, intriguing, special, or funny words. Your words can be long or short. They can be hard or easy to spell. After each word, use context clues in the text and reference materials to define the word.

- _____
- _____
- _____
- _____
- _____
- _____
- _____
- _____
- _____
- _____

Directions: Respond to these questions about the words in this section.

1. In chapter 4, Leslie **ominously** looks at Jess. Describe how she looks at him.

_____

_____

2. How is Miss Edmunds's manner **melodic**?

_____

_____

Analyzing the Literature

Provided below are discussion questions you can use in small groups, with the whole class, or for written assignments. Each question is given at two levels so you can choose the right question for each group of students. Activity sheets with these questions are provided (pages 28–29) if you want students to write their responses. For each question, a few key discussion points are provided for your reference.

Story Element	■ Level 1	▲ Level 2	Key Discussion Points
Plot	When does Jess decide to change his mind about Leslie?	Why does Jess change his mind about Leslie?	Jess decides to change his mind about Leslie when they are in Miss Edmunds's Friday music class. Singing and being around Miss Edmunds causes Jess to be in a good mood so he smiles at Leslie and decides to change his mind about her.
Plot	How do students react to learning that Leslie does not have a television at home?	Why does not having a television cause more problems for Leslie?	Students are shocked to learn that Leslie does not have a television. This is another way that Leslie is different from the other students, and it's another excuse for students to pick on her.
Character	Who is Janice Avery?	Why does Janice Avery bully other students?	Janice Avery is a bully who picks on younger, smaller kids. She picks on other students because she is bigger than them and because everyone is afraid to stand up to her.
Setting	What is Terabithia? Explain how Jess and Leslie get to Terabithia.	How does Terabithia help Leslie and Jess at school?	Terabithia is an imaginative kingdom that Jess and Leslie create. They have to use a rope to swing across water to Terabithia. It allows Jess and Leslie to escape the boredom and bullying they face at school.

Name _____

Date _____

■ Analyzing the Literature

Directions: Think about the section you just read. Read each question and state your response with textual evidence.

1. When does Jess decide to change his mind about Leslie?

   _____

   _____

   _____

2. How do students react to learning that Leslie does not have a television at home?

   _____

   _____

   _____

3. Who is Janice Avery?

   _____

   _____

   _____

4. What is Terabithia? Explain how Jess and Leslie get to Terabithia.

   _____

   _____

   _____

   _____

Name _____

Date _____

▲ Analyzing the Literature

Directions: Think about the section you just read. Read each question and state your response with textual evidence.

1. Why does Jess change his mind about Leslie?

   _____

   _____

   _____

   _____

2. Why does not having a television cause more problems for Leslie?

   _____

   _____

   _____

   _____

3. Why does Janice Avery bully other students?

   _____

   _____

   _____

   _____

4. How does Terabithia help Leslie and Jess at school?

   _____

   _____

   _____

   _____

Name _____

Date _____

Reader Response

Directions: Choose one of the following prompts about this section to answer. Be sure you include a topic sentence in your response, use textual evidence to support your opinion, and provide a strong conclusion that summarizes your opinion.

Writing Prompts

- **Informative/Explanatory Piece**—Both Jess and Leslie feel different from their peers. How have you felt different from your peers? What advice would you give to Jess and Leslie about feeling different?
- **Opinion/Argument Piece**—Think about the problems Jess and Leslie have with Janice Avery. How do you think they should handle the situation in order to solve their problem? Explain with details and tell why they should fix the problem that way.

_____

_____

_____

_____

_____

_____

_____

_____

_____

_____

_____

_____

_____

Name _____

Date _____

Close Reading the Literature

Directions: Closely reread the last few pages of chapter 4. Start at the paragraph that begins with, "There was really no free time at school . . . ." Read through the end of the chapter. Read each question and then revisit the text to find evidence that supports your answer.

1. Based on the text, in what way does Jess wish to be more like Leslie in the classroom?

   _____

   _____

   _____

2. Use this section to explain how Jess describes and relates to Leslie's parents.

   _____

   _____

   _____

3. According to the text, how does Jess's family act whenever Leslie visits their home?

   _____

   _____

   _____

4. What text evidence helps the reader understand that Leslie's friendship helps to motivate Jess?

   _____

   _____

   _____

Name _____

Date _____

Making Connections–Social Studies

Directions: Leslie comes from a suburban school, and Jess's school is rural. Use the Venn diagram to compare and contrast the differences and similarities between these two schools.

Jess's Rural School   Leslie's Suburban School

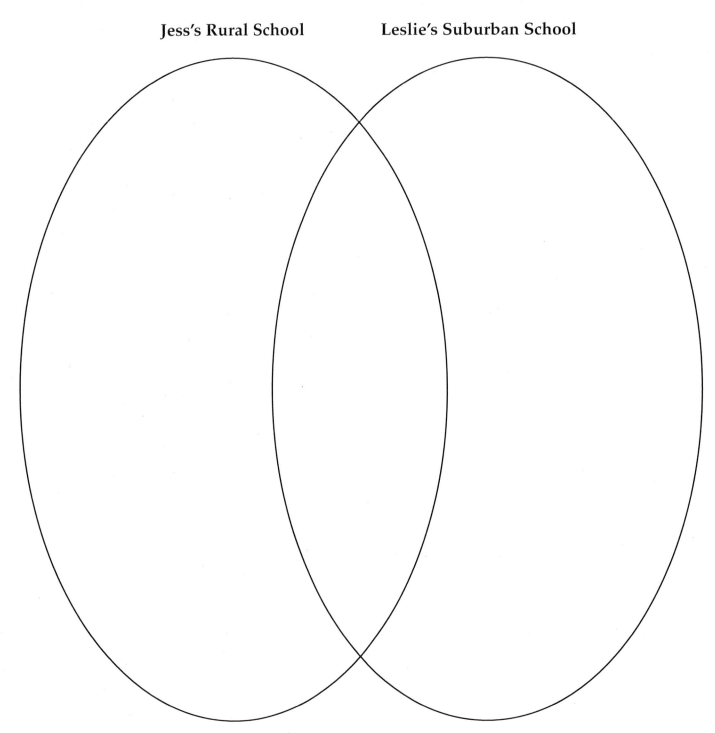

Name _____

Date _____

Creating with the Story Elements

Directions: Thinking about the story elements of character, setting, and plot in a novel is very important to understanding what is happening and why. Complete **one** of the following activities based on what you've read so far. Be creative and have fun!

Characters

Think about the situation that occurs between Janice Avery and Jess and Leslie. Create a comic strip to tell how the conversation might have gone if they would have confronted Janice Avery.

Setting

Create an aerial map of what Terabithia looks like. Be sure to include the rope swing, gully, and stronghold. Label your map.

Plot

Create a flow chart to show the incidents that unfold with Janice Avery, May Belle, Jess, and Leslie. Use arrows between events to show how each event led to the next event.

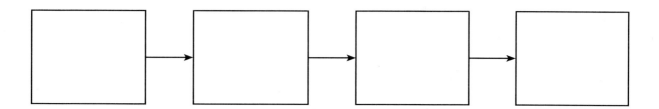

Vocabulary Overview

Ten key words from this section are provided below with definitions and sentences about how the words are used in the novel. Choose one of the vocabulary activity sheets (pages 35 or 36) for students to complete as they read this section. Monitor students as they work to ensure the definitions they have found are accurate and relate to the text. Finally, discuss these important vocabulary words with students. If you think these words or other words in the section warrant more time devoted to them, there are suggestions in the introduction for other vocabulary activities (page 5).

Word	Definition	Sentence about Text
foundling (ch. 6)	a child who has been abandoned	Jess hopes he is a **foundling** and not related to his older sister.
sneer (ch. 6)	to show scorn	Jess's older sisters **sneer** at Leslie's clothes every time she comes to their house.
splurged (ch. 6)	indulged	It is worth it to **splurge** on the doll for May Belle.
nuisance (ch. 7)	pest	Bill doesn't think Jess is a **nuisance** but rather useful and helpful.
realm (ch. 7)	kingdom	Jess and Leslie are the guardians of their **realm** deep within the forest.
vile (ch. 7)	awful; unpleasant	The **vile** Janice Avery is crying in the girls' bathroom, so Leslie decides to investigate.
complacent (ch. 8)	content	Miss Bessie is **complacent** and quiet as Jess quietly milks her.
obliged (ch. 8)	grateful; thankful	His father is **obliged** to find that Jess has finished milking the cow.
flounce (ch. 8)	prance; strut	Jess's older sisters **flounce** down the aisle at church in their new clothes.
gunnysack (ch. 8)	a bag made of burlap	Jess touches the old **gunnysack** as he talks with Leslie about God.

Name _____

Date _____

Understanding Vocabulary Words

Directions: The following words appear in this section of the novel. Use context clues and reference materials to determine an accurate definition for each word.

Word	Definition
foundling (ch. 6)	
sneer (ch. 6)	
splurged (ch. 6)	
nuisance (ch. 7)	
realm (ch. 7)	
vile (ch. 7)	
complacent (ch. 8)	
obliged (ch. 8)	
flounce (ch. 8)	
gunnysack (ch. 8)	

Name _____

Date _____

During-Reading Vocabulary Activity

Directions: As you read these chapters, record at least eight important words on the lines below. Try to find interesting, difficult, intriguing, special, or funny words. Your words can be long or short. They can be hard or easy to spell. After each word, use context clues in the text and reference materials to define the word.

- _____
- _____
- _____
- _____
- _____
- _____
- _____
- _____
- _____
- _____

Directions: Now, organize your words. Rewrite each of your words on a sticky note. Work as a group to create a bar graph of your words. You should stack any words that are the same on top of one another. Different words appear in different columns. Finally, discuss with a group why certain words were chosen more often than other words.

Analyzing the Literature

Provided below are discussion questions you can use in small groups, with the whole class, or for written assignments. Each question is given at two levels so you can choose the right question for each group of students. Activity sheets with these questions are provided (pages 38–39) if you want students to write their responses. For each question, a few key discussion points are provided for your reference.

Story Element	■ Level 1	▲ Level 2	Key Discussion Points
Character	Describe Leslie's interaction with Janice Avery in this section.	Why do Leslie's feelings change toward Janice Avery?	Leslie hears Janice Avery crying in the bathroom and goes in to talk to her. She learns that Janice's friends have shared private information with classmates, and this makes Leslie feel sorry for and act kindly toward Janice.
Character	How does Jess feel about Leslie?	Why does Jess want to give Leslie a great Christmas gift?	Jess cares about Leslie. He is proud to be her friend. He wants to show his gratitude and friendship toward Leslie with a thoughtful Christmas gift that will make her happy.
Setting	Describe Leslie's home environment.	How is Jess's home life different from Leslie's?	Leslie's home is filled with intellectual conversation between her parents. She doesn't have a television, so she talks with her parents and uses her imagination. Jess lives with four sisters and his mom and dad. It is always loud and chaotic, and someone is usually watching TV.
Plot	Why is it significant that Leslie goes to church with Jess and his family?	How does going to church affect Leslie?	Leslie has never been to church before because her parents don't go. Leslie thinks that church is better than a movie and that the sermon at church is interesting and beautiful.

Name _____

Date _____

Analyzing the Literature

Directions: Think about the section you just read. Read each question and state your response with textual evidence.

1. Describe Leslie's interaction with Janice Avery in this section.

_____

_____

_____

_____

2. How does Jess feel about Leslie?

_____

_____

_____

_____

3. Describe Leslie's home environment.

_____

_____

_____

_____

4. Why is it significant that Leslie goes to church with Jess and his family?

_____

_____

_____

_____

Name _____

Date _____

▲ Analyzing the Literature

Directions: Think about the section you just read. Read each question and state your response with textual evidence.

1. Why do Leslie's feelings change toward Janice Avery?

   _____

   _____

   _____

   _____

2. Why does Jess want to get Leslie a great Christmas gift?

   _____

   _____

   _____

   _____

3. How is Jess's home life different from Leslie's?

   _____

   _____

   _____

   _____

4. How does going to church affect Leslie?

   _____

   _____

   _____

   _____

Name _____

Date _____

Reader Response

Directions: Choose one of the following prompts about this section to answer. Be sure you include a topic sentence in your response, use textual evidence to support your opinion, and provide a strong conclusion that summarizes your opinion.

Writing Prompts

- **Narrative Piece**—Think about how Leslie helps Janice Avery. Describe a time when you have tried to help someone who did not treat you nicely. Explain why you decided to help that person in spite of how he or she treated you.
- **Opinion/Argument Piece**—When Jess spends time at Leslie's house helping her father, he finds that he enjoys it there. Based on the novel's descriptions, would you rather spend your time in Terabithia or at Leslie's house?

_____

_____

_____

_____

_____

_____

_____

_____

_____

_____

_____

_____

_____

Name _____

Date _____

Close Reading the Literature

Directions: Closely reread the first three pages of chapter 7. Read to the section where Leslie asks Jess why he hasn't been coming around. Read each question and then revisit the text to find evidence that supports your answer.

1. Use the novel to tell why Leslie has not been spending much time with Jess.

   _____

   _____

   _____

2. Based on the events in the novel, why is Jess unhappy with Leslie spending so much time with her dad?

   _____

   _____

   _____

3. Find text evidence to tell how Leslie's relationship with her dad differs from Jess's relationship with his dad.

   _____

   _____

   _____

4. Give evidence from the text to describe why Jess has stayed away from Leslie's house.

   _____

   _____

   _____

Name _____

Date _____

Making Connections–Items of Want Past and Present

Directions: My how times have changed! During this section of the novel we get to spend time with Jess's family during Christmas. He explains how much money certain presents cost, how much he gets to spend on his siblings, and what he wants for Christmas. Use the chart below to compare the costs of Jess's wish list items to gifts you'd like to receive.

Jess's List	Cost	My Wish List	Cost

Why do you think the cost of items has increased over time?

_____

_____

_____

_____

_____

_____

_____

Name _____

Date _____

Creating with the Story Elements

Directions: Thinking about the story elements of character, setting, and plot in a novel is very important to understanding what is happening and why. Complete **one** of the following activities based on what you've read so far. Be creative and have fun!

Characters

Create a Venn diagram. Use pictures or words to describe how Jess and Leslie are alike and different.

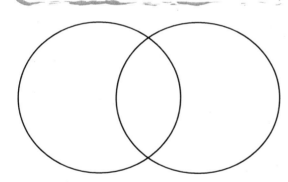

Setting

Create a picture of Jess's house and Leslie's house, side by side. Include labels to show what makes each house different from the other.

Plot

Think about what might happen next in the novel. Create a storyboard, and then write the next two pages of the story. Make sure you keep with the style of the novel.

Vocabulary Overview

Ten key words from this section are provided below with definitions and sentences about how the words are used in the novel. Choose one of the vocabulary activity sheets (pages 45 or 46) for students to complete as they read this section. Monitor students as they work to ensure the definitions they have found are accurate and relate to the text. Finally, discuss these important vocabulary words with students. If you think these words or other words in the section warrant more time devoted to them, there are suggestions in the introduction for other vocabulary activities (page 5).

Word	Definition	Sentence about Text
earnest (ch. 9)	serious; intense	The rain has been coming down in **earnest** for a couple of days, keeping Leslie and Jess from Terabithia.
plastered (ch. 9)	covered; stuck	Leslie's hair is **plastered** to her face as she seeks shelter from the rain.
sporadically (ch. 9)	irregularly; unpredictably	The rain has been falling **sporadically** for three days, making the creek bed overflow.
vanquished (ch. 9)	defeated; overpowered	Leslie and Jess send away their **vanquished** enemies.
discern (ch. 9)	determine	Leslie pleads for the ability to **discern** the spell that has kept the rain falling for so many days.
scrawny (ch. 10)	very thin	May Belle's **scrawny** body climbs back into bed as Jess leaves.
flank (ch. 10)	the side of an animal between the ribs and hip	Jess rests his head on Bessie's **flank** as he milks her.
absorbed (ch. 10)	consumed	May Belle is so **absorbed** in her cartoons she doesn't hear Jess leave with Miss Edmunds.
suppress (ch. 10)	control; overcome	Although he tries, Jess finds it difficult to **suppress** his smile when he sees Miss Edmunds.
vow (ch. 10)	promise; pledge	Jess makes a **vow** to himself to enjoy every detail of the landmarks he sees.

Name _____

Date _____

Understanding Vocabulary Words

Directions: The following words appear in this section of the novel. Use context clues and reference materials to determine an accurate definition for each word.

Word	Definition
earnest (ch. 9)	
plastered (ch. 9)	
sporadically (ch. 9)	
vanquished (ch. 9)	
discern (ch. 9)	
scrawny (ch. 10)	
flank (ch. 10)	
absorbed (ch. 10)	
suppress (ch. 10)	
vow (ch. 10)	

Name _____

Date _____

During-Reading Vocabulary Activity

Directions: As you read these chapters, record at least eight important words on the lines below. Try to find interesting, difficult, intriguing, special, or funny words. Your words can be long or short. They can be hard or easy to spell. After each word, use context clues in the text and reference materials to define the word.

- _____
- _____
- _____
- _____
- _____
- _____
- _____
- _____
- _____

Directions: Respond to these questions about the words in this section.

1. In chapter 9, the rain has **plastered** Leslie's hair to her face. Describe how she looks.

_____

_____

2. In chapter 10, May Belle is described as a **scrawny** girl. How does May Belle look?

_____

_____

Analyzing the Literature

Provided below are discussion questions you can use in small groups, with the whole class, or for written assignments. Each question is given at two levels so you can choose the right question for each group of students. Activity sheets with these questions are provided (pages 48–49) if you want students to write their responses. For each question, a few key discussion points are provided for your reference.

Story Element	■ Level 1	▲ Level 2	Key Discussion Points
Character	Why does Jess want to stay away from Terabithia until the rain stops?	In what ways does Jess verbally and nonverbally communicate his concern about the rising water?	Jess is afraid of the rising water, and he can't swim. He is concerned for the safety of him, Leslie, and the puppy. He wants to talk to Leslie about not going back to Terabithia until it stops raining and flooding.
Setting	Where do Jess and Miss Edmunds go in Washington, D.C.?	Why does Jess spend so much time at the Indian display in the Smithsonian?	Upon entering Washington, D.C., Jess and Miss Edmunds see monuments, landmarks, and the White House. They visit the Natural History Museum. The Smithsonian Indian display reminds Jess of his frightening drawings. Perhaps the display's artist would also understand Jess's drawings.
Setting	What has happened to the gully and surrounding lands that lead to Terabithia?	What evidence shows that Terabithia is not safe?	It has been raining on and off for days and the creeks and gullies are overflowing and flooding. Jess and Leslie can barely make it across the rope swing because the water is so high. The water is overflowing on the banks.
Plot	What does Jess find out when he returns from Washington, D.C.?	Why is Jess's mother so upset when he returns from Washington, D.C.?	Jess learns that Leslie drowned in the creek. His family was scared and worried because they thought Jess was with Leslie. No one knew he was with Miss Edmunds.

Name _____

Date _____

Analyzing the Literature

Directions: Think about the section you just read. Read each question and state your response with textual evidence.

1. Why does Jess want to stay away from Terabithia until the rain stops?

_____

_____

_____

_____

2. Where do Jess and Miss Edmunds go in Washington, D.C.?

_____

_____

_____

_____

3. What has happened to the gully and surrounding lands that lead to Terabithia?

_____

_____

_____

_____

4. What does Jess find out when he returns from Washington, D.C.?

_____

_____

_____

_____

Name _____

Date _____

▲ Analyzing the Literature

Directions: Think about the section you just read. Read each question and state your response with textual evidence.

1. In what ways does Jess verbally and nonverbally communicate his concern about the rising water?

   _____

   _____

   _____

   _____

2. Why does Jess spend so much time at the Indian display in the Smithsonian?

   _____

   _____

   _____

   _____

3. What evidence shows that Terabithia is not safe?

   _____

   _____

   _____

   _____

4. Why is Jess's mother so upset when he returns from Washington, D.C.?

   _____

   _____

   _____

   _____

Name _____

Date _____

Reader Response

Directions: Choose one of the following prompts about this section to answer. Be sure you include a topic sentence in your response, use textual evidence to support your opinion, and provide a strong conclusion that summarizes your opinion.

Writing Prompts

- **Opinion/Argument Piece**—Jess doesn't invite Leslie to go on the trip with Miss Edmunds. Put yourself in Jess's situation. Would you have made the same choice as Jess? Or, would you have included Leslie? Explain your decision.
- **Narrative Piece**—Think about how Jess's life may change after Leslie's death. Describe how Jess's life will be affected as well as his thoughts and feelings about these changes.

_____

_____

_____

_____

_____

_____

_____

_____

_____

_____

_____

_____

_____

_____

Name _____

Date _____

Close Reading the Literature

Directions: Closely reread the end of chapter 9 and the beginning of chapter 10. Start with, "She seemed satisfied." Read to the paragraph where May Belle tells Jess that Miss Edmunds is on the phone. Read each question and then revisit the text to find evidence that supports your answer.

1. Based on the text, why does Jess's father leave early in the morning even though he doesn't have a job?

   _____

   _____

   _____

2. What text evidence helps the reader understand why Jess is afraid to tell Leslie he doesn't want to go to Terabithia?

   _____

   _____

   _____

3. According to the text, in what ways is Jess's uneasiness about confronting Leslie similar to Miss Bessie's uneasiness around P.T.?

   _____

   _____

   _____

4. Using the novel as support, what solutions does Jess consider to overcome his fear of the water?

   _____

   _____

   _____

Name _____

Date _____

Making Connections—What If?

Directions: At the end of chapter 10, we learn that Leslie is dead. Think about how the novel would be different if Leslie were alive. What if Leslie was just waiting for Jess when he comes home from Washington, D.C.? What would Jess have done when he returned? What would he and Leslie do in Terabithia? How do you think the novel would have ended? Create an outline below. Then write at least one alternate chapter to the novel.

_____

_____

_____

_____

_____

_____

_____

_____

_____

_____

_____

_____

_____

_____

_____

_____

_____

Name _____

Date _____

Creating with the Story Elements

Directions: Thinking about the story elements of character, setting, and plot in a novel is very important to understanding what is happening and why. Complete **one** of the following activities based on what you've read so far. Be creative and have fun!

Characters

Create a chart that lists the reasons that Jess thinks of to overcome his fear of the water and also includes how Leslie might be able to help him with that fear. The chart should have reasons that are realistic of what we know about Leslie.

Setting

Use the Internet to find a map of Washington, D.C. Draw your own map of the area. Include the places that Jess and Miss Edmunds visit during their trip. Don't forget to use color and label each part of the diagram.

Plot

Think about how the trip to Washington, D.C. would be different if Jess brought Leslie. Rewrite chapter 10 with Leslie included on the trip.

Vocabulary Overview

Ten key words from this section are provided below with definitions and sentences about how the words are used in the novel. Choose one of the vocabulary activity sheets (pages 55 or 56) for students to complete as they read this section. Monitor students as they work to ensure the definitions they have found are accurate and relate to the text. Finally, discuss these important vocabulary words with students. If you think these words or other words in the section warrant more time devoted to them, there are suggestions in the introduction for other vocabulary activities (page 5).

Word	Definition	Sentence about Text
relentlessly (ch. 11)	persistently; without giving up	Jess runs **relentlessly**, hoping to outrun the pain.
hurtling (ch. 11)	forcefully throwing	Jess **hurtles** his paints into the rushing river.
accusation (ch. 11)	complaint; charge against someone	Jess fears his mother's **accusation** of not milking Miss Bessie.
smothering (ch. 12)	overwhelming	Ben's **smothering** hug greets Jess when he enters the room.
peculiar (ch. 12)	unusual	It is especially **peculiar** that even Brenda is being kind to Jess.
piteously (ch. 13)	pitifully; sadly	May Belle **piteously** looks at Jess after he smacks her.
constricting (ch. 13)	squeezing; pressing together	Jess's throat is **constricting** as he fights back emotions.
procession (ch. 13)	parade; demonstration to show respect	The **procession** for the queen of Terabithia is only seen by Jess and P.T.
traitorous (ch. 13)	disloyal	Jess feels **traitorous** for thinking about how he is now the fastest runner since Leslie is gone.
solemn (ch. 13)	sincere	May Belle makes a **solemn** promise to keep the secret about Terabithia.

Name _____

Date _____

Understanding Vocabulary Words

Directions: The following words appear in this section of the novel. Use context clues and reference materials to determine an accurate definition for each word.

Word	Definition
relentlessly (ch. 11)	
hurtling (ch. 11)	
accusation (ch. 11)	
smothering (ch. 12)	
peculiar (ch. 12)	
piteously (ch. 13)	
constricting (ch. 13)	
procession (ch. 13)	
traitorous (ch. 13)	
solemn (ch. 13)	

Name _____

Date _____

During-Reading Vocabulary Activity

Directions: As you read these chapters, choose five important words from the story. Use these words to complete the word flow chart below. On each arrow, write a word. In each box, explain how the connected pair of words relates to each other. An example for the words *procession* and *solemn* has been done for you.

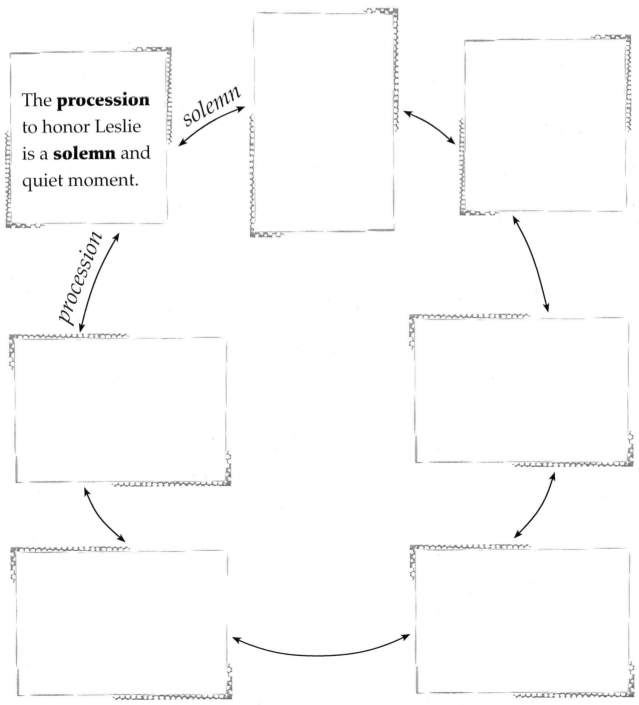

The **procession** to honor Leslie is a **solemn** and quiet moment.

Analyzing the Literature

Provided below are discussion questions you can use in small groups, with the whole class, or for written assignments. Each question is given at two levels so you can choose the right question for each group of students. Activity sheets with these questions are provided (pages 58–59) if you want students to write their responses. For each question, a few key discussion points are provided for your reference.

Story Element	■ Level 1	▲ Level 2	Key Discussion Points
Character	How does Jess react to the news about Leslie?	Why does Jess react the way he does to the news about Leslie?	Jess doesn't believe that Leslie is dead. He knows she was a good swimmer so he doesn't think it's possible. Jess is in denial about her death because that is how many people react to such a loss. It takes time for the news to sink in and become real to him.
Character	What does Mr. Aarons do to show he cares about Jess?	How does Jess's relationship with his father change after Leslie's death?	Jess's father follows him when he runs off after hearing the news about Leslie. He picks him up and holds him like a baby to comfort him. Jess's father comforts him and begins to speak to Jess like a grownup.
Setting	Explain how and what Jess uses to build a bridge into Terabithia.	What is the significance of Jess building the bridge to Terabithia?	At first Jess creates a bridge by putting a fallen tree across the water. Later, he creates a sturdier bridge out of boards. Building the bridge shows that Jess will continue to go to Terabithia even though Leslie is gone. It also represents how he will carry on in life without Leslie.
Plot	How does Jess introduce May Belle into Terabithia?	Why does Jess bring May Belle into Terabithia?	Jess brings his sister into the magical world of Terabithia to help keep Leslie's spirit alive; it's what she would have wanted. He also finds comfort in being able to mourn by being in that place.

Name _____

Date _____

Analyzing the Literature

Directions: Think about the section you just read. Read each question and state your response with textual evidence.

1. How does Jess react to the news about Leslie?

_____

_____

_____

2. What does Mr. Aarons do to show he cares about Jess?

_____

_____

_____

3. Explain how and what Jess uses to build a bridge into Terabithia.

_____

_____

_____

4. How does Jess introduce May Belle into Terabithia?

_____

_____

_____

Name _____

Date _____

▲ Analyzing the Literature

Directions: Think about the section you just read. Read each question and state your response with textual evidence.

1. Why does Jess react the way he does to the news about Leslie?

_____

_____

_____

_____

2. How does Jess's relationship with his father change after Leslie's death?

_____

_____

_____

_____

3. What is the significance of Jess building the bridge to Terabithia?

_____

_____

_____

_____

4. Why does Jess bring May Belle into Terabithia?

_____

_____

_____

_____

Name _____

Date _____

Reader Response

Directions: Choose one of the following prompts about this section to answer. Be sure you include a topic sentence in your response, use textual evidence to support your opinion, and provide a strong conclusion that summarizes your opinion.

Writing Prompts

- **Narrative Piece**—Imagine that you are in Jess's class. Think about what you would do or say to him after Leslie's death. Write a letter to Jess to share your thoughts and feelings.
- **Informative/Explanatory Piece**—Explain how returning to Terabithia will help Jess move on with his life.

_____

_____

_____

_____

_____

_____

_____

_____

_____

_____

_____

_____

_____

_____

_____

_____

Close Reading the Literature

Directions: Closely reread the last three pages of chapter 13, starting with, "Mrs. Myers had helped him already . . . ." Read each question and then revisit the text to find evidence that supports your answer.

1. Use text evidence to explain how Jess is adjusting to life after Leslie's death.

   _____

   _____

   _____

2. Use the novel to tell why nobody stays long at the Perkins place.

   _____

   _____

   _____

3. According to the text, how did Leslie help Jess understand what he is really capable of?

   _____

   _____

   _____

4. What text evidence helps the reader understand why Jess brings May Belle into Terabithia?

   _____

   _____

   _____

   _____

Name _____

Date _____

Making Connections—Make Believe

Directions: Terabithia is a magical, made-up place that Leslie creates to help her and Jess escape. Once she is no longer there, Jess struggles. What if Terabithia transformed into another magical place that could help Jess cope and grieve for his friend? Use the space provided to create, in pictures, another magical place just for Jess. You can come up with something completely new or use a magical setting from another novel (for example, Jess could travel to Hogwarts).

Creating with the Story Elements

Directions: Thinking about the story elements of character, setting, and plot in a novel is very important to understanding what is happening and why. Complete **one** of the following activities based on what you've read so far. Be creative and have fun!

Characters

Draw a picture of Leslie the way that Jess remembers her.

Setting

Write a poem that describes Terabithia at the end of the novel, in the spring and with the new bridge and a new queen.

Plot

Retell the ending of the story in cartoon or graphic novel format. Tell the story from the point of view of the citizens of Terabithia. How would they have felt about the return of their king and meeting their new queen?

Name _____

Date _____

Post-Reading Theme Thoughts

Directions: Read each of the statements in the first column. Choose a main character from *Bridge to Terabithia*. Think about that character's point of view. From that character's perspective, decide if the character would agree or disagree with the statements. Record the character's opinion by marking an *X* in Agree or Disagree for each statement. Explain your choices in the fourth column using text evidence.

Character I Chose: _____

Statement	Agree	Disagree	Explain Your Answer
People from different backgrounds can become best friends.			
There is no place for imagination in everyday living.			
People can overcome tragedies.			
Certain mistakes cannot be forgiven.			

Culminating Activity: Point of View

Katherine Paterson chose to write this story from the third-person point of view. It is a point of view in which the narrator is not a character in the novel, but the feelings and thoughts of a character or several characters are presented. In this narrative, the narrator shares only Jess's thoughts and feelings.

Directions: In the first row, write four different events from the novel. Then, use the novel to find evidence to describe Jess's thoughts or feelings about each event.

Event 1	Event 2	Event 3	Event 4
Evidence	Evidence	Evidence	Evidence

Name _____

Date _____

Culminating Activity: Point of View (cont.)

Directions: When your third-person point of view chart is complete, select one of the culminating projects below to complete.

- Imagine that you will create a play based on the novel. Design a poster for your *Bridge to Terabithia* play that depicts one of the events listed on your chart. Those who view this poster should be able to get a clear understanding of the lead character's point of view. The poster should also create excitement for your play.

- Choose a character from the novel. Use a significant event that happened to that character to create a third-person narrative of the event. Be sure to share the character's thoughts and feelings about that particular event.

- Choose a major event from the chart and create a reader's theater script. Be sure to include enough detail so a performance of the script will give the audience a sense of Jess's thoughts and feelings. Have a few of your classmates join you and give a presentation to the rest of the class.

Name _____

Date _____

Comprehension Assessment

Directions: Circle the best response to each question.

1. What is the meaning of the word **Terabithia** as it is used in the novel?

   A. a disease Leslie caught from being in the woods

   B. a magical place that Leslie and Jess create

   C. a four-legged insect found crawling on Miss Bessie

   D. a part of the school where only big kids could visit

2. Why does Jess dislike Leslie at first?

   E. She doesn't have a television in her home.

   F. She doesn't dress like any of the other girls do.

   G. She beats him during the races at recess.

   H. She doesn't want to play with the girls, just the boys.

3. There are many similarities and differences between Jess and Leslie. Record a detail for each bullet point in each section on the Venn diagram.

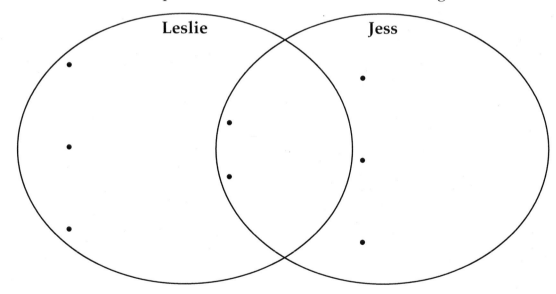

4. Which **two** details listed below could be in the middle section of the Venn diagram above.

   A. plays a trick on Janice Avery

   B. hates school

   C. finds a friend

   D. gets along with Mrs. Myers

Comprehension Assessment (cont.)

5. Which statement best expresses an overall theme of this novel?

    E. Never stand up to a bully, especially for what you believe in.

    F. Boys are better at most things than girls.

    G. Make-believe and magical places are for little kids.

    H. Friendship can be found in the least likely of people.

6. Which detail is the best evidence to support your answer to question 5?

    A. ". . . and Jess and I are going to figure out a way to pay her back for it."

    B. "It was Leslie who had taken him from the cow pasture into Terabithia and turned him into a king."

    C. "He could hear the third grade boys screaming him on. They would follow him around like a country-music star."

    D. "He put the flowers in her hair and led her across the bridge."

7. What are two differences between the Burke family and the Aarons family?

_____

_____

_____

_____

_____

_____

_____

8. Which statement below also shows a difference between the Burkes and Aarons?

    E. Jess enjoys being friends with his parents.

    F. Both Jess and Leslie's moms do not work outside the home.

    G. Leslie's family does not own a television set.

    H. Jess and Leslie both have a great deal of chores to do.

Name _____

Date _____

Response to Literature: Differences

Overview: *Bridge to Terabithia* has an underlying theme in this story regarding culture and community.

- Leslie's family comes from a suburban area where both parents work and make a good living. Leslie's family interacts with each other and are very close.

- Jess's family lives in a rural area where most families struggle financially, children are expected to help out around the farm, and there isn't always enough money or food to go around. His family is not very close. He hardly has a relationship with his father, and his mother is more engaged with the television than her children.

Directions: Think about these questions:

- Why is there a difference between the rural community where Jess lives and the suburban community from where Leslie came?

- If Jess's family had money, would everything be different for them, or would they be the same?

- Why would Leslie and her family move to a place so different from where they came?

Write an essay based on the answers of the preceding questions. Be sure to include evidence from the text. Your essay should follow these guidelines:

- **State a clear opinion.**

- **Be at least 750 words in length.**

- **Include answers to all questions asked.**

- **Draw upon, directly or indirectly, from *Bridge to Terabithia*.**

- **Provide a conclusion that summarizes your point of view.**

Name _____

Date _____

Response to Literature Rubric

Directions: Use this rubric to evaluate student responses.

	Exceptional Writing	Quality Writing	Developing Writing
Focus and Organization	☐ States a clear opinion and elaborates well. Engages the reader from the opening hook through the middle to the conclusion. Demonstrates clear understanding of the intended audience and purpose of the piece.	☐ Provides a clear and consistent opinion. Maintains a clear perspective and supports it through elaborating details. Makes the opinion clear in the opening hook and summarizes well in the conclusion.	☐ Provides an inconsistent point of view. Does not support the topic adequately or misses pertinent information. Provides lack of clarity in the beginning, middle, and conclusion.
Text Evidence	☐ Provides comprehensive and accurate support. Includes relevant and worthwhile text references.	☐ Provides limited support. Provides few supporting text references.	☐ Provides very limited support for the text. Provides no supporting text references.
Written Expression	☐ Uses descriptive and precise language with clarity and intention. Maintains a consistent voice and uses an appropriate tone that supports meaning. Uses multiple sentence types and transitions well between ideas.	☐ Uses a broad vocabulary. Maintains a consistent voice and supports a tone and feelings through language. Varies sentence length and word choices.	☐ Uses a limited and unvaried vocabulary. Provides an inconsistent or weak voice and tone. Provides little to no variation in sentence type and length.
Language Conventions	☐ Capitalizes, punctuates, and spells accurately. Demonstrates complete thoughts within sentences, with accurate subject-verb agreement. Uses paragraphs appropriately and with clear purpose.	☐ Capitalizes, punctuates, and spells accurately. Demonstrates complete thoughts within sentences and appropriate grammar. Paragraphs are properly divided and supported.	☐ Incorrectly capitalizes, punctuates, and spells. Uses fragmented or run-on sentences. Utilizes poor grammar overall. Paragraphs are poorly divided and developed.

The responses provided here are just examples of what students may answer. Many accurate responses are possible for the questions throughout this unit.

During-Reading Vocabulary Activity—Section 1: Chapters 1–3 (page 16)

1. Jess **despises** his sisters because of how they treat him. His older sisters used to dress him up and push him around in a doll carriage. They also don't have to do any chores and constantly pick on him.

2. Leslie is the only girl to enter the race, so she is **conspicuous**.

Close Reading the Literature—Section 1: Chapters 1–3 (page 21)

1. Leslie tries to talk with Jess, and he wants nothing to do with her. On the bus, he tries to avoid sitting with her and then runs home after getting off of the bus.

2. Leslie has a wide smile and shining eyes to show her happiness.

3. Jess wants nothing to do with Leslie. He's upset and frustrated with why she would ever want to race, and he wonders why she didn't play on the upper field with all the girls.

4. Jess doesn't qualify to the run the final race, but he doesn't want Gary Fulcher to win. He challenges Fulcher to let Leslie run so she can beat him.

Making Connections—Section 1: Chapters 1–3 (page 22)

The posters could include Jess milking Miss Bessie, tidying up his bedroom, and doing any other chores around the house. It could also show Jess running with a smile on his face.

During-Reading Vocabulary Activity—Section 2: Chapters 4–5 (page 26)

1. Leslie looks at him in a threatening way.

2. Miss Edmunds is very kind and enjoyable to listen to. Students enjoy her singing voice because it is **melodic**.

Close Reading the Literature—Section 2: Chapters 4–5 (page 31)

1. Leslie always appears to be a good student, even when she's daydreaming or thinking silly things about Mrs. Myers. Jess is always caught when he's daydreaming because it shows on his face.

2. Leslie's parents are writers. Jess doesn't think they look rich. They are nice to him, but he feels uncomfortable when they start talking about politics or fancy music.

3. Whenever Leslie is visiting Jess, his mother acts stiff, his sisters stare, and after she leaves his older sisters call her his girlfriend and make fun of her clothes.

4. Jess enjoys getting up every morning because he has something to look forward to. He sees Leslie as someone who is exciting and fun.

Making Connections—Section 2: Chapters 4–5 (page 32)

Jess's rural school: no money, no cafeteria, no air conditioner, no playground equipment, and no field trips

Leslie's suburban school: plenty of money, new computers, small class sizes, and field trips

Similarities: children, recess, learning

Close Reading the Literature—Section 3: Chapters 6–8 (page 41)

1. Leslie's dad is trying to fix up the old Perkins' place. He needs Leslie to help him find the tools he misplaces or help with the projects.

2. Jess is sad that Leslie is busy because it is taking away from the time he gets to spend with her. He tries to go into Terabithia alone, but it isn't magical without Leslie.

3. Leslie speaks of her father as a friend; one with whom she shares stories and laughs. Jess sees his dad as an authoritative person; someone he must obey or else he gets in trouble.

4. Jess has been afraid that her father would see him as someone who is in the way.

During-Reading Vocabulary Activity—Section 4: Chapters 9–10 (page 46)

1. Leslie's hair is stuck and covering her face because it is wet from the rain.
2. May Belle is very skinny.

Close Reading the Literature—Section 4: Chapters 9–10 (page 51)

1. He leaves to look for a job or to wait at the unemployment office.
2. Jess is disgusted with himself for being scared. He doesn't think a king would be so scared.
3. Jess and Miss Bessie are both uneasy and scared.
4. Jess plans to ask Leslie to teach him how to swim. He also thinks that scuba diving or having a "gut transplant" could help.

Close Reading the Literature—Section 5: Chapters 11–13 (page 61)

1. He often thinks of her and what she might do or say. He helps her parents pack their house and move out. He uses some of the old lumber from her house to build a bridge across the gully that connects to Terabithia. He introduces May Belle as the new queen.
2. The Burkes move out after their daughter dies. People have better places to go, to run to, or to run from.
3. Leslie makes Jess see that he is capable of more than he believes. He is a great friend, and she helps him see he is talented and creative.
4. Jess wants May Belle to see this world beyond the one they live in. He wants to teach her to dream and to pretend. He also wants to keep Leslie's spirit alive.

Comprehension Assessment (pages 67–68)

1. B. a magical place that Leslie and Jess create
2. G. She beats him during the races at recess.
3. The following facts could be included:
   - **Jess:** quiet, reserved, not adventurous, reserved around his family, loves drawing
   - **Similarities:** students in the fifth grade, believers in Terabithia, imaginative, wear jeans, play in the mud, activists for those who are treated unfair
   - **Leslie:** free spirit, friendly, talkative, doesn't wear dresses (unless to church with Jess), enjoys telling stories
4. Two details: A. plays a trick on Janice Avery; C. finds a friend
5. H. Friendship can be found in the least likely of people.
6. B. "It was Leslie who had taken him from the cow pasture into Terabithia and turned him into a king."
7. The Burkes are both writers who are wealthy, they are free-spirited, and they don't own a television. They also enjoy their relationship with their daughter and enjoy time with her. The Aarons are hardworking people who live off the land. They are reserved with their children.
8. G. Leslie's family does not own a television set.